Portfolio Building Activities in Social Media

Sara Miller McCune founded SAGE Publishing in 1965 to support the dissemination of usable knowledge and educate a global community. SAGE publishes more than 1000 journals and over 800 new books each year, spanning a wide range of subject areas. Our growing selection of library products includes archives, data, case studies and video. SAGE remains majority owned by our founder and after her lifetime will become owned by a charitable trust that secures the company's continued independence.

Los Angeles | London | New Delhi | Singapore | Washington DC | Melbourne

Portfolio Building Activities in Social Media

Exercises in Strategic Communication

Karen Freberg
University of Louisville

Los Angeles | London | New Delhi
Singapore | Washington DC | Melbourne

FOR INFORMATION:

SAGE Publications, Inc.
2455 Teller Road
Thousand Oaks, California 91320
E-mail: order@sagepub.com

SAGE Publications Ltd.
1 Oliver's Yard
55 City Road
London EC1Y 1SP
United Kingdom

SAGE Publications India Pvt. Ltd.
B 1/I 1 Mohan Cooperative Industrial Area
Mathura Road, New Delhi 110 044
India

SAGE Publications Asia-Pacific Pte. Ltd.
3 Church Street
#10-04 Samsung Hub
Singapore 049483

Printed in the United States of America

Library of Congress Cataloging-in-Publication Data

Names: Freberg, Karen June, author.

Title: Portfolio building activities in social media : exercises in strategic communication / Karen June Freberg.

Description: Los Angeles, California : SAGE, [2018]

Identifiers: LCCN 2018008493 | ISBN 9781544338255 (pbk. : alk. paper)

Subjects: LCSH: Internet marketing. | Internet in publicity. | Internet in public relations. | Social media. | LCGFT: Problems and exercises. | Textbooks.

Classification: LCC HF5415.1265 .F735 2018 | DDC 659.20285/4678—dc23
LC record available at https://lccn.loc.gov/2018008493

This book is printed on acid-free paper.

Acquisitions Editor: Terri Accomazzo
Editorial Assistant: Sarah Wilson
Production Editor: Bennie Clark Allen
Copy Editor: Melinda Masson
Typesetter: C&M Digitals (P) Ltd.
Proofreader: Annie Lubinsky
Cover Designer: Janet Kiesel
Marketing Manager: Liz Thornton

18 19 20 21 22 10 9 8 7 6 5 4 3 2 1

DETAILED CONTENTS

1

INTRODUCTION TO SOCIAL MEDIA: AN ART AND SCIENCE

These exercises can be done as take-home assignments or implemented in class (individuals and groups).

Social media is both a science and an art, so it is important to emphasize the creativity of what can be accomplished using social media. Creativity is a process, and this exercise will help in creating more opportunities to formulate your own vision of what creativity means to you, but also for how it can be applied in a social media context. It is important not only to have a great idea, but to be able to execute it effectively and strategically.

Describe what social media means to you visually. How would you describe social media visually? Pick one of the following creative options to help you share how you would define social media:

- Draw what social media means to you (hand or computer).

- Create a 3 × 3 grid (nine total boxes) and choose nine emojis that represent your view of social media.

- Make a social media mood board (like fashion designers do) or collage on what comes to mind when you think of social media.

- Create a 15-second video (using Adobe Spark Video or another mobile app video) showing what social media means to you.

Think of how social media can help solve a big problem or opportunity. In your opinion, what big problem facing the world can social media address? Use your imagination when considering how social media can help address and solve this problem.

Implement new ideas for how to use social media. Pick a company, nonprofit, or brand that is known for a platform (Facebook, Pinterest, Twitter, etc.). Describe how the company, nonprofit, or brand is using this platform, and propose a *new* and innovative way to use it.

SELF-AWARENESS EXERCISE

This exercise will gauge how students perceive their overall expertise and understanding of the field of social media. Provide this exercise either before the semester begins or during the first class.

NOTE: Review the answers at the end of the semester with the Self-Reflection and Actualization Exercise in Chapter 13 to see if there is a difference for the students.

Have the students watch Gary Vaynerchuk's self-awareness video, available from www.youtube.com/watch?v=j6tKf1IR5j8 (but be aware of language).

- How would you define social media? List several attributes that come to mind.

- How would you characterize yourself as a social media user?

- How would you characterize yourself as a social media strategist? Provide evidence and support for your answer.

- On a scale from 1 (*not at all*) to 5 (*completely*), how self-aware are you about your social media work? Discuss how this applies to what Gary Vaynerchuk highlighted in his video.

- What do you consider to be your strengths in your understanding of social media? What are your challenges?

- What are some takeaways you hope to get from this class?

- During this class, we will do several exercises and assignments. How confident are you that you will be able to master each of the following?
  - The content for the class
  - Assignments
  - Exercises on- and offline
  - Presentations (class clients, group presentations, individual presentations, client presentations, etc.)

- How confident are you in the content for this class? What areas are you most concerned about? List these and explain. Discuss also what steps you will take to address these challenges during the class.

- What are three goals you have for this class and beyond?

2 ETHICAL AND LEGAL FUNDAMENTALS OF SOCIAL MEDIA

SOCIAL MEDIA CODE OF ETHICS ASSIGNMENT

For this assignment, you are asked to outline and discuss the current state of social media ethics, but also what core principles you will follow as a social media professional.

For this assignment, make sure to outline each of the following:

- *The current state of social media ethics.* What trends are happening in the industry? What are two current cases to note related to social media ethics? Outline the current code of ethics for social media by two professional organizations you are interested in joining.

- *Brands/professionals with strong social media ethical codes.* What brands are utilizing proper social media ethical practices? Are there any professionals you feel practice strong ethical behavior on social media? Explain your choice with evidence. What are some takeaways you can bring forth in your own practices?

- *Key concepts and issues.* What main concepts do you feel are necessary to adhere to for your own personal conduct online?

- *What to do and not do.* What concepts or behaviors do you feel strongly against and want to make sure you avoid on social media?

- *Write a one-page outline* to use as your personal social media code of ethics. Include the 5–10 core concepts you will follow as a practicing social media professional. Provide at least five citations to articles and resources for this outline.

SOCIAL MEDIA POLICY ASSIGNMENT

You have been asked to create a social media policy for a

- New startup
- Business in town
- Student agency on campus
- Other (get approval by the professor)

In this assignment, you will need to

- *Define a social media policy (in three or four paragraphs).* What are social media policies used for? What are some of their main components? Outline and highlight two examples of social media policies by a brand, nonprofit, or agency.

- *Provide a brief overview* (in two or three paragraphs) of the client you will focus on for this social media policy.

- *State the client's use of social media (in two or three paragraphs).* Does the client have a social media policy? If so, does it need to be updated? Make sure to provide your rationale for where the client is at currently.

- *Propose a social media policy* for the client (two pages max). Outline the key activities and characteristics you would recommend the client follow. Discuss also how this will be implemented, reported, and analyzed in terms of whether or not it was successful.

Resources:

- Boudreaux, C. (2015). Social media policy database. *SocialMediaGovernance.com*. Retrieved from http://ow.ly/6xJP30eTREG

- Russell, J. (2017, July 27). How to write a social media policy for your company. *Hootsuite*. Retrieved from http://ow.ly/i6yf30eTRB9

3 PERSONAL AND PROFESSIONAL BRANDING

MANAGING ONLINE REPUTATION ASSIGNMENT

One of the important elements of being a social media professional and practitioner is being aware of not only your corporate or business online presence, but also your own online presence as an individual and professional in advertising and public relations.

For this assignment, you are asked to write a reflection paper (three to four pages max) covering the following material:

- *Overview:* Discuss your overall goals for your online reputation management practices for this class and beyond.
  - Some examples include establishing credibility and trust as a resource in a social media community on a specific topic or in a specific industry, engaging in an online community by sharing expertise and knowledge, getting mentions and other references on blogs from others, and managing a proactive reputation to obtain a job after graduation.
  - Make sure to state specific objectives that you have set in regard to your online reputation management efforts not only for this class, but also for after the class (internship opportunities, jobs, graduate school, etc.).

- *Personal reputation online overview:* Discuss and analyze your online bio presented through social media sites—blogs, Facebook, Twitter, LinkedIn, Pinterest, Snapchat, Instagram, YouTube, and so on. This includes providing a bio that you list on each of these sites. This can be visualized through a table in your paper.

- *Online reputation monitoring and analytics:* Reflect on your overall traffic and mentions on blog posts, Facebook, retweets, followers on Twitter, LinkedIn, Instagram, Pinterest, connections, and so on.
  - How many mentions on your blog, comments, or site visits over the course of this semester have you had so far?
  - What has the overall traffic been like on your blog since the beginning of this class?

- *Reflections on online reputation building:* Discuss how your blog and the information you share with others through social media enhance your online reputation—both personally and professionally.

  - Discuss the characteristics you possess that have helped build your online reputation (personality characteristics, information-sharing behavior, engaging consistently and professionally with followers and others through social media, etc.).

  - Think about future trends and goals for your online reputation for the rest of the semester, once you graduate, and beyond.

  - What were your perceptions before and after this assignment in regard to online reputation management?

- *Other:* Items to include in your paper as an appendix include (1) a list of profiles on social media, (2) tables and screenshots displaying social media traffic or influence via social media, and (3) tables listing URLs and profiles of social media outlets (e.g., Facebook, Twitter, LinkedIn, Instagram, Snapchat, and blogs).

While managing your online reputation is key, you want to also allow your students the opportunity to establish their own personal networking brand. This is one thing students want to know—how to get connected to professionals and the right people in the industry.

You may want to give out the following personal brand checklist to your class to work through and answer. Sharing these insights along with the reputation management paper will be very beneficial and enlightening for students.

Professors may also be interested in doing this for themselves.

PERSONAL BRANDING AND NETWORKING FRAMEWORK

One of the hardest (and most rewarding) efforts for social media professionals is to establish their personal brand as well as build their own personal learning networks and community. This is a checklist for you all to review, implement, and evaluate during the course.

1. IDENTIFY YOUR PERSONAL BRAND

- Who are you as a person?
  - What is your story? What makes you "you"?
  - What is your background? What are your hobbies and interests?
  - What key experiences, perspectives, and expertise do you bring to the table?
  - What are your strengths and weaknesses?
  - What steps are you going to take to improve your skills?
- What is your professional passion?
  - What personal qualities and characteristics make you unique?
  - How are you different from other students taking a social media class?
  - What steps are you going to take to achieve your ideal personal branding status?
  - What three, four, or five topics will you focus on to establish your thought leadership in the community, in the profession, and on social media?
- What overarching theme or message do you want brands, practitioners, and professionals in the industry to know?
  - What main areas of expertise do you want professionals to know you have?
  - What three industries or specializations do you want to identify with?
  - Construct your own lists of professionals, brands, blogs, Twitter handles, and others you want to engage with online:
    - Lists of influencers in the industry you want to work in
    - Lists of agencies, brands, and companies you want to work for
    - Lists of professionals you're inspired to be like when you graduate
    - Lists of internship and job opportunities
    - Lists of chats to participate in your particular industry
  - Follow others mentioned among those you respect and admire in your community:
    - Brands
    - Professionals

- Influencers
- Community leaders
- Businesses
- Nonprofit organizations

2. IDENTIFY GOALS AND OVERALL PROFESSIONAL PURPOSE

- Identify your personal brand voice.
  - What is your purpose in the field, and what can you offer that is different from others?
  - What is the overall tone of your social media voice? In what ways are you going to show this to the community?
  - What steps do you want to take to achieve your goals? Which people do you want to connect with online who can mentor, educate, and be part of your community?
- Be aware of professional actions on social media.
  - Be humble and be generous.
  - Always think before you post.
  - Ask for feedback and responses from your community. Use Twitter polls for questions if you want.
- Pay it forward.
  - Think about the people you want to reach, and by sharing innovative and timely resources, you will start attracting an audience and become listed as a "must-follow" in your community.
  - Practice curation strategies.
    - Share each other's work. The best way to get more traffic is to increase exposure and awareness of your work.
    - Give credit to the original users.
    - Provide a comment, feedback, or takeaway for every post.
  - Share content such as
    - Blogs
    - Resources
    - Tutorials
    - Lists of best practices
    - SlideShares
    - Videos and podcasts

3. ESTABLISH A PERSONAL BRAND

- Visual
  - Create a consistent visual branding of yourself.
  - Fit the picture, professionalism, cover page, and background to the platform.
  - Present the same bio and voice across social media platforms.
- Content
  - Create, curate, and connect online. Share new content on a regular basis from blogs, websites, news outlets, and relevant chats you participate in.
  - Mix up the content you share. Use Ow.ly and Hootlet to share content in real time or at a scheduled time or day.
  - Share original content on a regular basis.
  - Provide a mixture of original and curated content.
  - Think about what questions, problems, or issues people in your industry want answers to—consider sharing content that could answer these questions or solve these problems. Be a resource.
- Engagement
  - Monitor engagement and interactions. See what content is shared or engaged with more than others.
  - Respond in a timely manner, listen to what people are saying, and implement proper social media etiquette techniques.
  - Showcase your personality.
- Voice
  - Be confident in your voice and perspective while being respectful toward others.
  - Monitor and listen to what others say about you. Reflect and analyze on a regular basis.
- Comment on and acknowledge content from others.
  - This can be done via the quote feature on Twitter.
  - Images and videos are key. Make sure to include images (personalized through branding sites like Canva) along with your links and comments).
  - Give out congrats and shout-outs.

4. STAY INFORMED AND CONNECTED

- Be informed.
  - Follow relevant brands, industry outlets, and blogs that cover the topics you are interested in.
  - Follow relevant professionals working in the industry you want to work for.

- Become connected.
  - Find Twitter chat sessions (e.g., #SMSportsChat, #BufferChat, and #HootChat) for your respective topics.
  - Start a dialogue and conversation.
  - Make it easy to connect and be part of your community.

5. ESTABLISH (AND SUSTAIN) YOUR PERSONAL NETWORK

- Sustain your community connection.
  - Connect with fellow professionals and start the conversation.
  - Read and respond to/share content from professionals, bloggers, and practitioners you respect.
  - Share relevant, new, and innovative campaigns or resources you feel your network may want to look at.
  - Seek out mentors in your profession. Connect, engage, and correspond to build professional relationships.
  - Give shout-outs on a regular basis (not all of the time) to those you respect and share why.
  - Give thanks to those who provide you with shout-outs.
  - Conduct virtual introductions.
  - Find those whom you want to mentor and help.
- Share blog posts with a class hashtag.
  - Post blog post content on LinkedIn Pulse.
  - Comment and share updates you enjoy or want to give a shout-out to.
  - Share updates on a regular basis, but don't spam or blast followers too much.

SOCIAL MEDIA COACHING AND THOUGHT LEADERSHIP REPORT

In this course, you will learn about the different elements of a personal social media brand and persona online.

However, while you will explore how to manage your own personal brand, this assignment focuses on developing a plan for *two people* by helping them with social media. You will have to get permission from the professor for this assignment during the second week of the semester.

This assignment will allow you to get experience in not just understanding the importance of personal branding for yourself, but also teaching others how they can manage, create, and promote their own personal brand. This consulting exercise will help you get a start in helping others, which will prepare you as you enter the workplace and may be looked to for assistance in this area of social media.

Assignment Format:

- Present this as a white paper or e-book. Consider exploring tools such as Adobe Illustrator and visual templates to best articulate your message. Think of your own personal brand—how do you want to present yourself as a social media professional?

ASSIGNMENT OVERVIEW

- *Executive Summary.* This is the last thing you will write—a one-page overview of the report, whom you focused on for your coaching and thought leadership, and then a summary of suggestions and ideas.

- *Introduction.* Discuss the current state of social media, define thought leadership and social media coaching, and identify key trends in this area. Address also the growing expectation that professionals have consulting experience and clients to establish presence in the industry.

- *Overview of Clients.* Provide a brief biographical background of the clients. Provide a strategic rationale for why you have focused on each person (e.g., small business owner, start-up business, event or nonprofit organization you are volunteering for). Family, friends, and significant others do not count *unless* there is a business or strategic purpose. If this is the case, consult with the professor.

- *Social Media Audit.* You will need to do *two* social media audits for these professionals. Follow the guidelines outlined on the next page to complete your analysis.

- *Goals and Objectives.* Identify the strategic implication for each client, and then discuss your overall objectives and goals to get them *known* on social media. Make sure they are consistent with the SMART (specific, measurable, achievable, realistic, and time-specific) criteria for objectives.

- *Opportunity to Address for Social Media Coaching.* Provide the *background of two people* you would like to help coach on social media and provide guidance on a subject or area of focus in social media (personal branding, developing a Facebook advertising campaign, getting started with live video for storytelling, crisis communication for social media training, etc.). Discuss challenges and obstacles that need to be addressed to make sure the social media coaching goes well.

- *Propose Strategies and Tactics.* Based on your recommendations, you will need to identify how to make these people's social media presence more effective based on the area you have chosen. Possible areas to offer social media coaching on include

  o   Personal branding

  o   Social media writing

  o   Social media analytics

  o   Specific platform-based help (Instagram, Snapchat, etc.)

  o   Content planning and creation

  o   Video

  o   Recommendations for tools, programs, and educational certifications the two people may need to invest in or take in social media

- *Measurement.* Have a list of deliverables you will give to the two professionals in this report along with key steps they need to take to continue with these social media efforts after your consultation. Explain the evaluation metrics you will have them report to you about in a timeline. Discuss also what next steps to take based on this coaching exercise.

- *Summary.* Provide five takeaways from the experience and a summary of personal branding and thought leadership. Write up the report and summary of the two consulting opportunities.

- *References.* Please provide at least five to seven references to support the points, resources, and research you share in this report.

- *Appendix.* You need to create at least *three* mockups of proposed tactics for each client (a total of six) based on your recommendations.

SOCIAL MEDIA CERTIFICATIONS AUDIT REPORT

Many certification programs are available for social media marketing and strategic communications. The challenge, of course, is deciding which one to invest in, and which one to have as part of your résumé and curriculum vitae. Your task for this assignment is to review all of the certifications for digital marketing. Review those that are platform based (Facebook, Twitter, etc.) and others that are sponsored by brands. In addition, research and identify at least three new emerging certifications you would invest in or watch for. After reviewing all of the certifications, their features and benefits, and the overall cost, make sure to provide your recommendations on which certifications you need to invest in, and which are necessary for getting into the field.

SOCIAL MEDIA CERTIFICATIONS	Host Company	Types of Certifications	Rationale for Certification	Features	Cost	Importance of Being Certified With This Program
PLATFORM BASED	Facebook					
	Twitter					
	Instagram					
	LinkedIn					
	Other: _____					
BRAND	Hootsuite	• Hootsuite Academy • Advanced Social Media Strategy • Social Advertising				
	HubSpot	• Content Marketing • Social Media • Inbound Marketing				
	Google	• Google Analytics • Google AdWords				
	BrandWatch	• Brandwatch for Students				
	Other: _____					
EMERGING CERTIFICATIONS (NEW)						
RECOMMENDATIONS						

KEY AREAS OF SOCIAL MEDIA TREE

You are asked to create a key areas of social media tree for what you want your personal brand to be. These topics are what you can speak on proficiently and are passionate about. These topics can be platform or channel based (Facebook, YouTube, Instagram, etc.), industry specific (public relations, marketing, journalism, etc.), or strategy/area based (influencer marketing, analytics, content creation, storytelling, etc.).

Ask yourself the following questions:

- What am I passionate about?

- What are some topics I have experience talking about?

- What are natural areas I can talk about?

- What subtopics are related to the main topic categories?

- What format can I use to talk about these topics? Examples include
    - Educational materials (workshops, tutorials, webinars, white papers, e-books, etc.)
    - Personal branding (conference presentations, guest blog posts, interviews, etc.)
    - Content creation pieces (blog posts, vlogs, infographics, etc.)

ACTIVITY/ASSIGNMENT

- Create a key areas of social media tree for yourself. Outline the main topic areas and then *three* subtopic areas within the topic trees.

- Propose *three formats* in which you can talk about the area (one for each subtopic).

- Provide a rationale for why you feel this topic is a good one to focus on for your personal brand. In addition, note why you have chosen the specific formats in which to talk about these topics.

- Outline the next three steps you will take to accomplish these tasks.

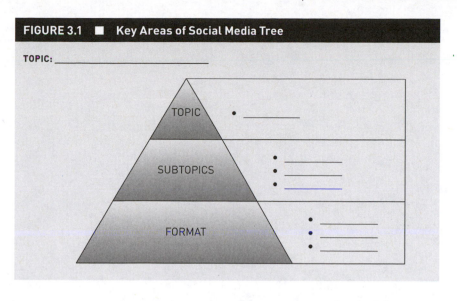

FIGURE 3.1 ■ Key Areas of Social Media Tree

TOPIC: _____

Rationale for Topic: _____

_____

_____

_____

_____

_____

_____

_____

_____

Rationale for Format: _____

_____

_____

_____

_____

_____

_____

_____

Next Steps I'll Need to Take: _____

_____

_____

_____

_____

_____

_____

_____

4 INDUSTRY QUALIFICATIONS AND ROLES

You are asked to provide an overview of the current state of the social media profession for class. Your responsibility is to identify three potential jobs you want to apply for and analyze them based on certain components. You will then be asked to decide what position you will be applying for, and how you will approach this task.

Create a report (one to three pages single spaced) on your analysis for each job.

OVERVIEW OF THE ASSIGNMENT

Positions can be chosen by looking at the job postings on certain sites (MEOjobs, etc.) or from brands themselves (BuzzFeed, Bleacher Report, Twitter, Facebook, etc.).

Make sure to discuss the following:

- *Current employment state.* What is your overall goal—to get an internship or job? In what areas are you interested in working in social media?

- *Overview of the job postings* you have chosen. Outline the three job postings you have chosen, and have a rationale for why you have chosen these.

- *Similarities and differences.* What experiences, skills, and responsibilities are similar for all of these jobs? What are some of their differences?

- *Job requirements.* Outline the key certifications, programs, and tools each job states as key components to be knowledgeable on. Outline which ones you have, and others you will work toward getting more experience in.

- *Decision and next steps.* Which job did you decide to apply for? Provide your rationale. Outline five steps you will take to apply for this job.

- *Content creation.* Create three pieces of content you will need to have in place before you apply for this position.
  - *Some examples include* LinkedIn Note, Adobe Spark Cover Letter and Resume, Instagram Story Reel and Resume, an Adobe Premiere Video highlight reel to share on Twitter, and an infographic of your résumé.

- *References.* Provide your references with proper citations.

NETWORKING AND OUTREACH ASSIGNMENT

You want to get started in the industry, but you do not know where to start and whom to connect with. This exercise will prepare you to network on social media in a proactive and professional manner.

STEP 1: Identify the industry and area you want to get into.

- Research the industry and see who are the major players (companies, agencies, nonprofits, media outlets, etc.). What is the current state of this industry?

- Note the history, client work, and vision statement for the particular industry you are looking for. Why do you want to work here? What campaigns and social media activities are professionals in this industry doing that is working for them?

- Evaluate their social media accounts. Conduct a mini social media audit to see what they are doing well, and what they could improve on. Follow their social media accounts on all platforms.

- Research the current jobs outlined. What are some qualifications employers are looking for?

STEP 2: Research professionals.

- Research people you would like to connect with. Look to see if there are bios on the main website of the company, agency, or organization you are looking at. How did these professionals get to where they are today?

- Evaluate how they present themselves on LinkedIn and Twitter. Are they consistent? What are they sharing?

- Are there any connections, similarities, or experiences you share with these professionals?

- Outline the findings you have collected.

STEP 3: Draft initial outreach message and contact.

- Determine which platform would be best for reaching out to these professionals.

- Evaluate your own digital presence. Are you consistent and showing your true and authentic personal brand? How would others perceive your digital footprint? Revise and update if necessary to present the best and true first impression online.

- Draft an initial note (formatted for the platform) to connect with others.
  - Discuss why you are connecting with them.
  - Keep it short and to the point.

- ○ Don't go for the hard sell—talk about why you want to learn more about their journey and experience. Ask how they got to where they are today.

- ○ Edit, check for grammar and spelling, and edit again.

STEP 4: Reach out.

- Take the initial step to reach out to the professional.

- Determine what your objective is (connection, possible job shadow opportunity, meet for coffee, etc.).

- Evaluate the experience. What did you learn from this activity? What would you do differently? What are some best practices you learned in the process?

- Discuss next steps. What are some next steps you will be taking based on the experience you had here?

5 RESEARCH IN SOCIAL MEDIA: MONITORING, LISTENING, AND ANALYSIS

SOCIAL MEDIA INTERNAL AND EXTERNAL AUDIT ASSIGNMENT

In this assignment, you are asked to create an internal audit, external audit, and summary of recommendations for future social media practices for your respective university. This may take some time to complete, and it may be necessary to reach out to the social media team at your university. Listed as follows are the components you will need to complete and report on for this assignment.

1. INTERNAL AUDIT: You have been asked to review the social media activities for your university's social media presence. You will need to complete the following table and discuss in your analysis

   - *Background and history of the university.* What are some key characteristics, features, statistics, and points that would be important to note?

   - *Background of social media use internally.* Is the university on social media? If so, for how long, and what has it done with each platform?

	Background	Content and Rationale	Strengths and Weaknesses	Action Steps and Recommendations
Internal Communication				
Personnel and Team Analysis				
Education and Mentorship				
Employee/Student Social Media Policy/Advocacy Program				
Leadership				
Brand Voice				
Analytics				
SUMMARY				

2. EXTERNAL AUDIT: After doing the audit for the university's internal social media practices, it is time to conduct an external audit of what the university has done. Complete the table as follows and highlight some of the university's key activities, what platforms it is on, what type of content it has created and shared, and what is missing.

	Background	Brand Voice	Relationship/ Rationale	Content and Rationale	Strengths and Weaknesses	Action Steps and Recommendations
Platform						
Campaigns						
Influencers						
Community Analysis						
Content Creation/ Message Analysis						
Analytics and Data						
SUMMARY						

3. SUMMARY OF RECOMMENDATIONS: Based on your analysis of the internal and external social media activities, provide a summary of steps to take for future social media initiatives by the university. Provide at least three action steps and recommendations you would suggest the university take advantage of. In addition, share at least three educational resources or trainings you feel the university may benefit from in the future to help it in its social media practices.

BRAND SOCIAL MEDIA TEMPLATE ANALYSIS ASSIGNMENT

This assignment will give you some experience in analyzing companies that are doing social media well, what they are doing that is working, and what challenges and successes they need to address.

1. Choose a company to look at and analyze. You will need to outline what it is doing as far as social media goes, but also discuss some of its successes and challenges. Provide an overview of what the company has done so far on social media.

2. Pick two other companies associated with this company in the industry. Some examples include

    - Apple, Samsung, and Dell

    - NFL, MLB, and NBA

    - Wendy's and Arby's

    - SoundCloud and Spotify

    - Nike and Adidas

    - Bleacher Report and ESPN

    - Starbucks and Dunkin' Donuts

    - Coca-Cola, Pepsi, and Mountain Dew

    - Taco Bell, McDonald's, and KFC

3. Provide your recommendations for each company and what it is doing on social media for your strategic insights column.

4. Address any gaps. This is where you identify the missed opportunities, and possible directions in which the company can go for the future. Discuss the overall insights you gathered from this exercise here.

5. Provide your references for citations appropriately.

Company	Platforms	Content Voice Community	Organizational Structure	Campaign	Influencers	Share of Voice	Analytics	Successes and Challenges	Strategic Insights
Gaps to Address									

SOCIAL MEDIA PLATFORM ASSESSMENT ASSIGNMENT

You are asked to provide an overview of a social media platform for class. Your responsibility is to educate your fellow classmates on the history, trends and features, platform background, key case studies, crises that used this platform, campaigns that have used this platform, and future implications of the platform.

You will be asked to create a report (one to three pages single spaced) on the platform, of course. Each student will be asked to select a platform to analyze (first come, first served for platform choice!). Each entry will be collected and then incorporated into an e-book for the class on all of the social media platforms.

OVERVIEW OF THE ASSIGNMENT

Platforms to choose from should come from the Conversation Prism 5.0 (https://conversationprism.com/). Some platforms that are listed on the diagram include

- Facebook

- Instagram

- WhatsApp

- Snapchat

- Twitter

- LinkedIn

- YouTube

- Pinterest

- Weibo

- Line

- Other (ask professor for permission)

Make sure to discuss the following:

- *History and key trends of the platform.* When was the platform first launched? Who founded the platform? Who are the main competitors for features and audience members?

  ○ If you are covering Facebook or Twitter, discuss an international platform that is similar to it (e.g., Twitter and Weibo).

  ○ Discuss whether it is public or has been purchased by another company, and so on.

- *User information and statistics.* How many people are on the platform? You might want to either visit the platform's About Us page (e.g., www.facebook.com/pg/facebook/about/) or check out the latest report from We Are Social on global social media trends.

- *Platform's place in social media*. Where does the platform stand in the social media industry? Is it popular globally? In certain industries (entertainment, media, news, public relations, journalism, etc.)?

- *Analysis of media content*. What is being shared on this platform? How are users creating content here? What are the ways in which brands interact on the platform? Highlight a campaign that has been praised for using this platform successfully.

- *Unique characteristics and metrics*. What elements make this platform different from others?

- *Benefits and challenges*. What are the unique benefits of this platform? What are some of the positive ways brands, individuals, and others have used this platform? What are some challenges/risks you need to be aware of about the platform? Share one example of how this platform has been involved in a crisis and/or been at the forefront of creating new challenges for a brand, a person, or another entity.

- *Best practices*. Highlight five best practices for how to use this platform professionally and personally.

- *Do you use this platform* personally, professionally, or both? Provide your rationale.

- *What is your take on this platform for the future*? Will it stay successful? Will it fade out? What are three predictions you have here?

- *References*. Provide your references with proper citations.

SOCIAL MEDIA LISTENING ASSIGNMENT

In this assignment, you are asked to evaluate a brand, nonprofit, or account by using a social media listening tool.

Examples of listening tools include

- Brandwatch
- Hootsuite
- Sprout Social
- Buffer
- Sysomos
- Salesforce
- Meltwater
- Talkwalker
- Zoomph

OVERVIEW OF THE ASSIGNMENT/COMPONENTS

1. *Overview of the listening tool you will be using.* Discuss the tool's features, the main advantages and disadvantages, and the scope of time you will need to conduct this listening procedure.

2. *Overview of the client of focus.* Discuss briefly the account you will be analyzing and what it has done (and is not doing) on social media. Highlight what social listening tools the account is or is not using. In addition, highlighting what it is able to spend on social listening is key.

3. *Provide an overview* of the use of vanity metrics, channel metrics, advanced metrics, and behavioral metrics. Which ones will you use in this report, and why?

4. Overall *sentiment of the content* (what does it mean?) for all of the platforms. What channels are the most positive? Neutral? Negative? What does this say about the community using each of these platforms?

For Twitter specifically, make sure to report and *provide an overview of what this means for your client.*

- Twitter reach
- Twitter reach—mention type
- Twitter reach—engagement type
- Twitter reach—authority type

- Sentiment

- Mentions

- Most retweeted

- Top trending hashtags

- Provide at least two recommended additional metrics not listed here that you feel would be key to note.

- Make sure to note the sentiment, mentions, users, and communities on Twitter for your analysis.

5. *Communities and influencers.* For influencers, report and analyze the top sources and the most authoritative, top influencers.

   - Screen capture their communities' network *and* discuss what the communities mean for the client.

   - Outline and discuss key influencers you feel your client needs to reach out to that would be relevant and necessary in this campaign. When you are discussing these influencers, make sure to (1) analyze them, (2) outline their audience, and (3) note their community and network. How is this relevant for your brand?

6. *Competitive analysis.* Run a comparison of the competitors of attractions that are competing with your brand and related to your overall goal for your campaign. You will need to include at three competitors in this analysis for this section, but you are welcome to do more.

   - Utilize the filters for this. Make sure to focus on certain areas and locations for this project.

   - Look at what the community online is saying about these attractions. How is the overall sentiment? Who are the main influencers? What does your community look like online? What hashtags are people using to share their experiences on Instagram while at these attractions?

7. *Recommendations and strategic insights.*

   - What are the main findings from this analysis?

   - What insights can you use to determine what the client needs to do for your group's social media campaign?

   - Organize findings and statistics found from data collected in your SWOT (strengths, weaknesses, opportunities, and threats) analysis.

SOCIAL MEDIA "RIFF-OFF" COMPETITION

This exercise is inspired by the movie *Pitch Perfect*. Gather the students into groups and formulate teams. Each team has to create updates in real time based on the topics at hand to try to be as relevant as possible for its personal brand in real time. Brands have been able to do this well in some cases (e.g., Wendy's and MoonPie), but others have not. To be a successful social media professional, you may need to improvise with your brand voice on social media when appropriate.

Each team competes and follows the rules of the "riff-off" competition. Each member is responsible for coming up with a social media update (Twitter may be best for this) and share this with the class. If a student is stumped or his or her update is not appropriate (not relating to brand, topic, etc.), the team is out of the competition. Once a team is out, the next topic is chosen. The last remaining team wins!

Each student group has to focus on one brand. The students have to research and find out their brand voice, what they have posted on their social media accounts, and if they have done anything like this before.

Suggested brands include the following examples, but can be personalized based on the interest of the class:

- Pepsi

- MoonPie

- Charmin

- Cinnabon

- Coca-Cola

- Arby's

- Taco Bell

- Wendy's

- KFC

Example topics for the social media "riff-off" include the following (you can make a spinner with the topics):

- Star Wars Day (May the 4th Be With You)

- Halloween

- National Coffee Day

- Oscars

- Mother's Day

- National Cookie Day

- Back to School

- National Pet Day

- Ditch Your Resolution Day

- National Best Friend Day

- Other holidays to celebrate on social media (see, e.g., https://blog.hootsuite.com/weird-holidays-to-celebrate-on-social-media/)

6 STRATEGIC PLANNING FOR SOCIAL MEDIA

As discussed in Chapter 11 ("How Social Media Is Applied"), one of the areas in which social media is used frequently is crisis communication.

Social media can help crisis communicators

- Disseminate information in a timely manner

- Increase the potential impact of key messages in a crisis or noncrisis situation

- Leverage the networks of community members to make the information easier to share with others (employees, team members, media, community residents, etc.)

- Personalize each message for a designated audience and channel

- Engage and interact with audiences in real time

For this assignment, you will need to prepare *a social media crisis communication plan* for a client of your choice. Outline the following details in your plan:

- *Overview of the business, nonprofit, agency, or start-up you are focusing on.* What industry is the client in? What are its products and services? Who is part of the team?

- *Analysis of social media channels.* Conduct a brief social media audit. List what channels the client is using on social media, and analyze what types of content, voice, and information it has on these sites.

- *Review any potential crises experienced in the client's history.* Which ones were the most damaging? If the client has not experienced a crisis, outline at least three potential crises it could potentially face.

- Once you have identified the crises, *identify what steps and platforms* to take in order to address this situation. Consider exploring the possibility of proposing
  - Monitoring and listening simulation exercises with social media
  - Creating a crisis team

- ○ Preparing training and education workshop sessions on social media and crisis communication

- ○ Key words, metrics, and tools you would want the client to use for social media and crisis communication efforts

- Discuss briefly how you will determine if this social media crisis plan has been successful, and recommend what the client needs to do after the crisis.

SWOT ANALYSIS ASSIGNMENT

You are about to interview with the company of your dreams for a summer social media internship, and you have to do your research ahead of your interview.

- *Overview of the company.* Discuss this company and why you want to interview with it. What has the company done on social media that really inspires you? Who oversees social media at the company? What is their background, and what initiatives have they taken on social media (campaigns, new partnerships, news articles and features, awards, etc.)? Do they hire an outside agency for their creative work?

- *Brand voice.* What is the company's brand voice? What characteristics would you use to describe its overall content, tone, and community on social media? Outline two or three of the company's recent efforts on social media.

- *SWOT analysis.* Look at the company's current campaigns and channels and discuss its strengths, weaknesses, opportunities, and threats (SWOT) as a brand on social media. Highlight social media campaigns the company has implemented in the past. Use analytics (e.g., vanity metrics, analysis of content, which audiences the company is reaching, and whether or not it has influencers, bots, or key professionals as followers) in your analysis.

- Create a visual with these insights, and then a rationale summarizing why you have listed each point. Include at least two or three references for *each* section (if you use 3 references each, that's 12 references total) to back your rationale with evidence.
    - Strengths
    - Weaknesses
    - Opportunities
    - Threats

- *Strategic implications.* Last, write two or three strategic implications the company needs to note for future social media campaigns. Focus on how you will present these data in your interview (video, infographic, SlideDeck presentation, etc.).

- *References.* Make sure your references are properly cited.

STRATEGIC BRIEF

You want to provide a wide range of assignments for your students to practice with. One of the assignments I love giving my students involves a specific social media strategy.

This allows them to pick a new platform, platform feature, or tool (e.g., Instagram Stories) and propose how a business, client, or organization locally could use this proactively.

Keep the following in mind when you are looking at particular strategy assignments:

- *Be very clear on your expectations.* Make sure you clearly articulate what you are looking for in this particular assignment.

- *Provide an opportunity for students to test their creativity.* State that they can't look at what other brands or companies have done.

- *Tie this into multiple approaches.* You can assign this as part of a client project or individually as well.

- *Provide platform resources for assignment.* With a new platform (e.g., Snapchat), add a few references at the end of the paper for additional readings that may be helpful for your students when working on this assignment.

- *Tie this into a timed exercise.* Sometimes we are asked on the spot what to do creatively and strategically for a brand using a new platform. This can be easily tied into a timed writing exercise.

Overview

You are asked to propose a strategic storytelling brief for either

- Your client for class

- A local business or brand (corporate, small business, nonprofit, event, etc.)

- Yourself (how would you use it professionally to get a job with the brand/agency/company of your dreams after graduation?)

Some ideas for how to use this platform or new tool strategically for a brand (or individual persona) include using promotional videos, contests or sweepstakes, behind-the-scenes footage, selfies, unveiling of new products or campaigns, exclusive content from events, and introduction to team members or special guests.

PAPER FORMAT (MAX TWO PAGES, SINGLE SPACED)

- *Introduction to tool or platform* (who started this app, statistics of users and number of active users on the app, how it's been used, prominent campaigns and brands using the app, etc.). Make sure to cite references to these figures.

- *Overview of your company/brand.* Is it using this platform or tool? Is there a rationale for your company/brand to be on this platform or use this tool? Why or why not?

- *Key audiences* (who you are targeting). Demographic and psychographic insights are key to point out here for this particular audience.

- *Strategic mindset* (key motivational points, interests, trends, and issues you would want to know about your audience members—what are they thinking right now, and what do we want them to think or do after this campaign [call-to-action steps]?). What is the *story* you want to communicate and share with this audience?

- *Objectives* (what is the overall objective to accomplish with this initiative?).

- *Strategies* (how are we going to accomplish our objectives, and with what resources and communication tools or tactics?). Make sure to have at least three strategies with two tactics.

- *Optional.* You are more than welcome to create some snaps for your assignment to showcase your story or propose storyboard snap ideas. Make sure you consider best practices and proper etiquette when doing this for this assignment. This can be part of your appendix section and not part of the maximum two pages.

- *Etiquette and proposed best practices* for using Snapchat.

- *References* (all in APA [American Psychological Association] style).

TIPS

- Make sure you connect the audience with the overall goal and application.

- Be creative. Look at the possibilities out there for using this particular app for your company or the brand you have chosen.

- Be aware of both positives *and* negatives of the brand. Consider the additional implications and best practices brands and social media professionals must be aware of when it comes to this app. You may want to address this in proper etiquette as well as suggesting a Snapchat professional guide.

SOCIAL MEDIA EVENT PLANNING
CONTENT GAME PLAN ASSIGNMENT

You are asked to create a social media event planning content game plan for a local tourism event. Your task is to create content for a week out of the event.

Pick a local event (holiday, parade, game, festival, etc.) for which you would like to plan social media content.

OVERVIEW OF THE COMPONENTS FOR THIS ASSIGNMENT

- *Overview of the event that will be covered.* Outline its background, history, and connection to the community.

- *Brand voice on social media.* What is the overall tone for the event's social media accounts? What has the tourism board done previously in the past?

- *Previous social media coverage of events.* What has the tourism board done before? What worked or did not work? What are some opportunities and new tools to test out?

- *Analysis of content.* How frequent were the posts about the event? What times worked and did not work for the event? Explore the metrics and data needed to see what days/times and platforms performed the best.

- *Content strategy and execution overview.* Provide a list of the overall estimates for timing for the event, which platforms will be used, how many pieces of content will be shared on each platform, content that will be shared, the overall brand voice, and who will be responsible. *Note:* You will need to do a separate list for each platform you use (e.g., if you use Facebook, Instagram, and Snapchat, you will need to create three of these tables).

- *Content game plan for the event.* Create your proposed calendar and game plan for the event. Highlight the platforms that will be used (based on your analysis of the event's previous social media platforms) and the pieces of content you want to share out at certain times.

- *Measurement and evaluation.* Discuss what metrics you will use to determine whether or not this is effective for the event on social media.

- *Bonus.* Reach out to the event and propose this content calendar. Discuss the possibility of taking over the tourism board's account for the event to get hands-on experience managing, creating, and evaluating the content for the event.

CONTENT STRATEGY AND EXECUTION OVERVIEW TEMPLATE

Time	Platform	Number of Pieces of Content	Content and Theme	Brand Voice	Who Is Responsible

CONTENT GAME PLAN TEMPLATE (EXECUTION AND TIMING OF CONTENT)

Sunday		Monday	Tuesday	Wednesday	Thursday	Friday	Saturday
7:00 a.m.	* Content Highlighted						
10:00 a.m.							
12:00 p.m.							
2:00 p.m.							
4:00 p.m.							
6:00 p.m.							

7 STRATEGIC WRITING FOR SOCIAL MEDIA

CREATING A STYLE AND WRITING GUIDE ASSIGNMENT

1. You are asked to create and launch a style and writing guide for your internship (and/or future employer). Choose an agency, brand, or company you want to work for. Research and evaluate its style guide to determine if anything needs to be added or changed as far as the writing and visual style goes.

2. You are tasked with creating your own style and writing guide on social media. Reflect on how you want to present yourself and some key elements you want to keep consistent across the different channels.

For either assignment, you will need to outline

- Writing style

- Voice and tone

- Content types

- Content elements

- Visual elements (brand kit, colors, typography, etc.)

- Guidelines and best practices

Examples include the following:

- MailChimp: https://styleguide.mailchimp.com/voice-and-tone/

- New York University: www.nyu.edu/content/dam/nyu/cmsTeam/documents/socialmedia/NYU_SocialMedia_StyleGuide_092914.pdf

- Cisco: www.cisco.com/c/m/en_us/about/brand-center/copyright-use/copyright-material-guidelines/interactive-brand-book.html

- Others: www.canva.com/learn/50-meticulous-style-guides-every-startup-see-launching/

BLOGGING ASSIGNMENT

Presently, one of the more established forms of online media among advertising and public relations professionals is the blog. Some professionals even consider blogs to be more like traditional media. This semester, you will create your own personal blog where you are asked to write posts relevant to course material, current events in the industry, and other topics of interest to you.

A blog should be an interactive, current, and engaging platform where you can demonstrate your visual, written, and creative expertise about a particular subject of interest. This is also a place where you can share your insights and education with the online community.

Your blog will allow you to showcase your knowledge and experience in advertising and public relations, while also reflecting a positive, energetic, and dynamic reputation as a young professional/student.

For professors, I strongly recommend setting up a blog as well if you haven't done so already. Students react if they have to do an assignment that the professor doesn't have to do. Medium, WordPress, and Blogger are just a few platforms that are very user friendly and easy to set up. Make sure you understand the expectations of what students are going through with this assignment, but remember that it provides an outlet for your own content creation as well (helping your overall reputation as a social media professor).

Here are some tips to note about blogging:

- Make sure your posts are professionally written—grammar and spelling are key since they are the first thing people will judge you on.

- Make sure to share your blog posts with the class (use Bitly to shorten the URLs) and attach a hashtag to the update on Twitter.

- Make sure to reference the articles and pictures/videos you use in your blog post. Include at *least three hyperlinks to articles or videos in each of your blog posts.*

- Keep blog posts to no more than 500 words.

- Be generous with your insights and information—make sure to include links to articles, videos, reports, and podcasts that enhance and support the points in your post.

- Have a title for your post that is unique and creative and catches the attention of your reader to go on to your post.

- Tag your posts with key search terms—if you are writing about a particular subject (e.g., social media and ethics), make sure that you tag your post with these key terms so they appear in search engines.

- *Remember: You cannot use copyrighted material.* You can only link to content.

As far as the assignment goes, how many posts the students should write is up to the professor. Here is what I have my students do for my social media class:

You are asked to write *two blog posts* a week. You are more than welcome to write more if you like. *Extra credit* will be provided for students who write blog posts related to the guest lectures for this class (review syllabus for schedule):

- One post will be dedicated to a social media topic or trend that we are discussing in class that week or that you find interesting related to strategic communications.

- The other post will be dedicated to what you are passionate about or interested in (a particular industry, hobby, nonprofit cause, etc.). The topic is up to you—but be aware that what you post on your blog is available publicly for others to see.

Some additional ideas to consider for blog posts include the following:

- Lists (e.g., best social media resources or must-follows for public relations on social media)

- Best practices (tips for Instagram, Vine, or another social media platform)

- Case studies

- New resources or emerging trends

You must complete your two blog posts and share them via Twitter using the class hashtag by [deadline]. Lateness or failure to produce a blog post for the week will be noted, and point deductions will be made.

You will need to

- Provide me with your blog URL from Twitter by using the class hashtag.

- Share each of your blog posts (copy the URL in your tweet update) on Twitter using the class hashtag as well.

- Make sure you are prepared to share your blog posts in class each Monday. Students will be selected at random, so make sure you have completed your blog posts by the assigned deadline.

- *Note:* You will need to make sure *not* to post two blogs on the same day (e.g., Friday right before the deadline). These posts should be done throughout the week.

Blog topics can also be emphasized and tailored for the class. You can follow the same guidelines set forth in your Twitter policy, or you can do it a little differently. I try to do the same content and allow students to write at a deeper level in their blogs using some of the resources shared online.

Also, make sure to share blogging etiquette and ethics so students realize they have to make sure to be transparent and up front with their views with others. Morten Rand-Hendriksen has a great resource to cite and share with your students:

Blogger Ethics

1. It is your right to voice your opinion.

2. Be critical of everything, even yourself.

3. Use your power to protect.

4. Tell the truth at all times.

5. Present your opinion as your opinion.

6. State your allegiances to stay independent.

7. Reveal your sources unless doing so can harm your sources.

8. Be critical of your sources and seek independent verification.

9. Always give credit where credit is due.

10. Always preserve the intended meaning of a given statement.

11. Give your opponent a chance to respond.

12. Admit and disclose your mistakes immediately.

Source: Rand-Hendriksen, M. (n.d.). Code of ethics for bloggers, social media and content creators. *MOR10*. Retrieved from https://mor10.com/code-of-ethics-for-bloggers-social-media-and-content-creators/

COMMUNITY COPYWRITING ASSIGNMENT

You are invited to be part of the interview process for a social media community content creator and manager role. The company you are working for is Converse. You are asked to create content for the company on social media based on the images presented. Write down the copy you would write for each image based on your understanding of the brand, and provide a rationale for why you wrote the copy for each image.

Note: All images are part of Creative Commons and are free to use.

PLATFORM	IMAGE	COPY *What copy would you write for these images?*	RATIONALE *Why did you approach this copy this way?*
FACEBOOK	A		
	B		
	C		
TWITTER	A		

(Continued)

Sources: Photo A, Arman Zhenikeyev/Getty Images; Photo B, Smith Collection/Getty Images; Photo C, Ren_Zemanek/EyeEm/Getty Images.

(Continued)

PLATFORM	IMAGE	COPY *What copy would you write for these images?*	RATIONALE *Why did you approach this copy this way?*
	B		
	C		
INSTAGRAM	A		
	B		
	C		

Sources: Photo A, Arman Zhenikeyev/Getty Images; Photo B, Smith Collection/Getty Images; Photo C, Ren_Zemanek/EyeEm/Getty Images.

INFOGRAPHICS ASSIGNMENT

ASSIGNMENT OVERVIEW

You are asked to create an infographic explaining a concept or topic of interest within strategic communications (advertising, public relations, etc.). Infographics are based on research and data, so make sure you find reports and statistics to support these points and cite them in APA (American Psychological Association) format.

COMPONENTS FOR INFOGRAPHIC ASSIGNMENT

1. *Infographic Social Media Strategy Brief:* Write one page maximum discussing the overall purpose and goals of the infographic for the client.

Provide the following information: a brief bio of the client (three to four sentences), the goal of the infographic, SMART (specific, measurable, achievable, realistic, and time-specific) objectives for the infographic, audience targeting (employees, customers, social media bloggers, etc.), strategies on how to share this infographic, and metrics for evaluating the success of this infographic.

2. *Client Infographic:* Create an infographic for your client and focus on covering the basic business information in a visual and professional manner. Make sure to cover the following groups of information:
   - **Statistics** (sales, revenues, market research, surveys, etc.). Statistics help tell a story visually like engagement across social media platforms for the client.
   - **Process** (manufacturing, customer service, public relations, etc.). Discuss the various steps the client goes through internally as well as the internal process of customer relations for online communications/social media practices.
   - **Timeline** (company history, major campaigns, products and services launched, etc.)
   - **Ideas** (concepts, theories, vision statement, etc.)
   - **Geography** (locations, metrics by region and cities, etc.)
   - **Relationships** (audiences internally and externally, products and services, etc.)

Components of an effective infographic: Make sure to focus on (1) color scheme related to the brand and client focused on in this project; (2) use of graphics and visuals to illustrate data and information; (3) strategic use of charts and graphs; and (4) type of font.

3. *Research:* For your infographic, you will need to provide additional research to support your points. References to research from the Pew Research Center,

Nielsen, Altimeter Group, Edelman Trust Barometer, and others are examples to use and cite in your infographic.

4. *Blog post on infographic*: Once you have created your infographic, you will need to write a post (300 words max) on your personal blog about the infographic process. You may include lessons learned from this assignment, overall trends and uses of infographics in public relations, and additional resources you found useful for creating and learning more about infographics.

5. *Timeline:* You will need to have written this blog post by the time you turn in your infographic and infographic social media strategy brief.

Grading Rubric	Points
Infographic Social Media Strategy Brief	40
Infographic	40
Infographic Blog Post	20
Total	100

TIPS TO REMEMBER

- *Determine the overall purpose and rationale* for the infographic for your client. Think about what this infographic will do to communicate data/research/additional information to target audiences.

- *Mix the use of visuals and symbols into your infographic.* Think about symbols to illustrate some of your data (maps, gender, products, etc.) to help convey the story about your client visually.

- *Think about the target audience.* What audiences are you targeting on behalf of the client with this infographic? How will you market this strategically for this particular audience? Where will you share this (Facebook, Twitter, Visually, Pinterest, etc.).

- *Strategize about what data to use.* Where will the data and research come from? Pew Research Center, Public Relations Society of America, International Association of Business Communicators, and Altimeter Group are just a few examples.

- Make sure to reference statistics, facts, and additional research used in the infographic. These will be presented at the bottom of the infographic page as footnotes.

- *For design purposes, look for inspiration.* Visually, CoolInfographics.com and other infographic databases are good resources for ideas on what to do with your client infographic. However, you have to *create an original infographic and cite the resources appropriately.*

E-BOOK ASSIGNMENT

One of the hardest tasks in social media is to establish yourself as a thought leader in the industry.

Creating an e-book is one way to do this. Many social media agencies and brands (Digiday, Hootsuite, Sprout Social, HubSpot, etc.) have used e-books to educate, inform, and provide value to their audiences in a way that helps them achieve their goals. However, this process can be somewhat intense and, at times, turn into a larger project than originally anticipated.

This assignment will provide you with the opportunity to create your own e-book. Consider what topic you want to cover, explore, and write about.

COMPONENTS OF THE E-BOOK ASSIGNMENT

Here are the requirements for this assignment:

Components	Grade
Drafts of e-book (1 and 2)	20% (10% each)
Final draft of e-book	30%
Presentation	10%
Promotion materials	10%
Writing requirements (voice, clarity, grammar, spelling)	15%
Quality of research	15%
Total	100%

SCHEDULE FOR THE E-BOOK ASSIGNMENT

- Topic approval for e-book by the instructor (due Week 2)

- Outline of e-book with room for feedback by the instructor (due Week 4)

- Draft 1 to the instructor (due Week 6)

- Draft 2 with final revisions to the instructor (due Week 8)

- Design of the e-book with professional template and proposed promotions (due Week 10)

- Final version to be shared and presented to the class (due Week 12)

Along with creating the e-book, you will need to have the following ready to submit with this assignment:

- Ways you will promote the e-book. Provide two examples from the following:
  - Email newsletter
  - Landing page
  - Blog post
  - Infographic
- Sample mock-ups for social media updates you will create to promote the e-book along with a written copy for each update.
  - Facebook Creative Studios (Facebook and Instagram)
  - Twitter (Twitter Media Studio)
  - LinkedIn (Pulse article/ad)

TIPS TO KEEP IN MIND

- Make sure the copy in the e-book is edited, and check for spelling or grammar mistakes.

- Evaluate the key words and terms you are using so they are searchable online. Determine what key words you will be using for your e-book, but anticipate what key words others (those whom you want to reach with this e-book) will use to search for this piece of work.

- Integrate visuals into your e-book. Look at the design capabilities and make sure you outline what images need to be included (make sure to cite these images correctly and use Creative Commons images).

- Have strong call-to-action statements for the promotional materials you will use for your e-book.

RESOURCES FOR E-BOOKS

- Hussain, A. (2018, February 26). How to create an ebook from start to finish (Free ebook templates). *HubSpot*. Retrieved from http://ow.ly/ATke30eSBpb

- Canva. (2018). Design a professional-quality ebook online with Canva. Retrieved from http://ow.ly/h6I830eSBqx

ORGANIC VERSUS THIRD-PARTY TOOL EXERCISE

You are asked to record your social media activities for a week using both organic and third-party tools (Hootsuite, Buffer, Sprout Social, etc.) to post your updates. You are asked to report three posts you have shared organically (natively to the platform) and three you used a service to post (Hootsuite, Buffer, Sprout Social, etc.). This assignment was inspired by a Buffer experiment done by Brian Peters in 2017.

For this exercise, you will need to present and turn in the following information as an assignment:

- *Overview of your Facebook, Twitter, and Instagram presence.* Is it consistent, and what is the overall audience size for each platform? What is your brand voice on each of these platforms?

- *Social media behavior.* Do you already use any tools or services to post content on social media? If so, which ones?

- *Overview of the selected third-party tool.* Why did you choose this tool and not others?

- *Analysis of the process by which you approached this assignment.* What were some of the challenges and opportunities you saw? For each post, you need to report the post (describe whether it was a photo, GIF, text, or link), provide a link to the post, and then report key performance indicators, or KPIs (reach, engagement, reactions, etc.), specific to the platform. Please complete the following table with this information.

	Organic			Third Party		
Facebook	Post:	Post:	Post:	Post:	Post:	Post:
	Link:	Link:	Link:	Link:	Link:	Link:
	KPIs:	KPIs:	KPIs:	KPIs:	KPIs:	KPIs:
Instagram	Post:	Post:	Post:	Post:	Post:	Post:
	Link:	Link:	Link:	Link:	Link:	Link:
	KPIs:	KPIs:	KPIs:	KPIs:	KPIs:	KPIs:
Twitter	Post:	Post:	Post:	Post:	Post:	Post:
	Link:	Link:	Link:	Link:	Link:	Link:
	KPIs:	KPIs:	KPIs:	KPIs:	KPIs:	KPIs:

- *Key lessons from this experience.* Were there any surprises? What are your recommendations for the future?

- *References* (if needed to provide explanation for the results).

Keep each of the following in mind:

- Post your updates at different times (not all on the same day). Space them out throughout the week.

- Analyze their reach, engagement, and impressions. Note and report the time, context, and what you did that could have sparked a lot of engagement.

8 AUDIENCE SEGMENTATION AND ANALYSIS

You are asked to analyze three audiences for your university. Discuss each of the audiences in detail based on the following categories:

- Introduction to the audience group

- Demographics

- Psychographics

- Platform specifics

- Type of social media users

- Certain behaviors they have on social media (e.g., social media metrics)

- Content that resonates with them on social media

- Relationship
  - Discuss the current relationship these audiences have with the university offline.
  - Discuss the current relationship these audiences have with the university online.

- Recommendations for engaging with them on social media
  - Provide three ways you would recommend approaching this particular audience group on social media.

Audience Segmentation Characteristics

Demographics	Psychographics	Platform Specifics	Type of Social Media User	Social Metrics
• Age • Gender • Occupation • Race • Location • Language Preference • Relationship status	• Attitudes • Behaviors • Interests • Opinions • Lifestyle • Connections	• Life stage • Company size • Industry • Function/job • Type of user • Response to content • Loyalty to brand	• Creator • Inactive • Collector • Spectator • Critic • Joiner	• Specific digital behaviors on certain platforms • Likes/follows/interests • Time spent on platforms • Content that resonates with audiences on certain platforms • Device used • Other similar interests/brands they follow

AUDIENCE ANALYSIS WORKSHEET ASSIGNMENT

As described in Chapter 11 ("How Social Media Is Applied," Part I), it is important to note how to engage with audience members appropriately. Each audience member needs to feel that the message and content (as well as the exchanges through social care practices) is personalized and relevant.

This assignment will give you an opportunity to construct audience analysis profiles for how to approach different audiences, and what content will resonate with them. Choose three audiences for either (1) your class client, (2) a job or internship you are applying for, or (3) a brand. Outline and complete the audience analysis profile for these three audiences.

Audience 1

	Assessment and Audience Strategy
Name of Audience Group	
Key Audience Characteristics (demographics, psychographics, etc.)	
Relationship to Client	
Relationship to Social Media (platforms used, etc.)	
Interests	
Content • What types of content is this audience looking for on social media? • What types of reactions or behaviors does this audience have?	
Influencers/Micro-influencers and Opinion Leaders to Consider (provide background and rationale for each)	
Social Media Communities the Audience Is Involved In (groups, pages, Twitter chats, shows, etc.)	
What would make the members of this audience change their behavior or attitudes toward the client on social media?	
Key Messages	• Key Message 1 • Key Message 2
Supporting Facts	• Supporting Fact 1 • Supporting Fact 2
Steps to Take for Engagement and Interaction	
Content to Create to Engage With This Audience	
PESO (paid, earned, shared, and owned) Media to Consider	
Action Steps (What steps do you recommend taking to engage with this audience strategically?)	

Audience 2	
	Assessment and Audience Strategy
Name of Audience Group	
Key Audience Characteristics (demographics, psychographics, etc.)	
Relationship to Client	
Relationship to Social Media (platforms used, etc.)	
Interests	
Content • What types of content is this audience looking for on social media? • What types of reactions or behaviors does this audience have?	
Influencers/Micro-influencers and Opinion Leaders to Consider	
Social Media Communities the Audience Is Involved In (groups, pages, Twitter chats, shows, etc.)	
What would make the members of this audience change their behavior or attitudes toward the client on social media?	
Key Messages	• Key Message 1 • Key Message 2
Supporting Facts	• Supporting Fact 1 • Supporting Fact 2
Steps to Take for Engagement and Interaction	
Content to Create to Engage With This Audience	
PESO (paid, earned, shared, and owned) Media to Consider	
Action Steps (What steps do you recommend taking to engage with this audience strategically?)	

Audience 3	
	Assessment and Audience Strategy
Name of Audience Group	
Key Audience Characteristics (demographics, psychographics, etc.)	
Relationship to Client	
Relationship to Social Media (platforms used, etc.)	
Interests	
Content • What types of content is this audience looking for on social media? • What types of reactions or behaviors does this audience have?	
Influencers/Micro-influencers and Opinion Leaders to Consider	
Social Media Communities This Audience Is Involved In (groups, pages, Twitter chats, shows, etc.)	
What would make the members of this audience change their behavior or attitudes toward the client on social media?	
Key Messages	• Key Message 1 • Key Message 2
Supporting Facts	• Supporting Fact 1 • Supporting Fact 2
Steps to Take for Engagement and Interaction	
Content to Create to Engage With This Audience	
PESO (paid, earned, shared, and owned) Media to Consider	
Action Steps (What steps do you recommend taking to engage with this audience strategically?)	

AUDIENCE SEGMENTATION AUDIT ASSIGNMENT

You are asked to create an audience segmentation audit for your client, which is

- Your university
- A local business or nonprofit
- A local agency
- A local organization
- A brand

You want to analyze the client's social media coverage (e.g., Facebook, Instagram, and Twitter) and determine its (1) top influencers, (2) top creators, (3) ambassadors, and (4) trolls/haters (if any). Discuss the implications and impact of these audiences on the online reputation for your client. Provide recommendations for how to address these findings in your assignment.

COMPONENTS OF THIS ASSIGNMENT

- *Overview of the client.* Provide a concise overview of the focus for this assignment.

- *Description of the client's key audiences.* Who are the main audience members the client is trying to reach and engage with on social media?

- *Analysis of the client's influencers, creators, ambassadors, trolls, and haters.* Discuss key examples, characteristics, and situations or times where these audiences are engaging with the brand. What campaigns and other partnerships has the client done? What has been its success rate with its communities? Provide detailed results based on key performance indicators and measurements here. What have been the biggest opportunities and challenges among all of these audiences for the client?

- *Analysis of the messages.* How are these audiences connecting or talking about the brand? What type of social media content are they sharing? What is the overall sentiment and view toward the brand?

- *Recommendations.* Provide three recommendations for the client to engage with these audiences based on your analysis.

Influencers	Creators	Ambassadors	Trolls/Haters
• Leverage size of audience • Paid endorsements • Access to brands and events • Brands are in control of relationship for brand voice • One-way commitment	• Leverage opportunities for creativity • Paid endorsements • Partnership • Creators are in control of creativity execution • Two-way commitment/co-creation	• Leverage level of loyalty and commitment • Paid endorsements and exclusive access • Ambassadors are in control of amount of participation involved	• Leverage level of outrage and anger toward brands and communities • Constant interactions and comments • Tagging media outlets for recognition of actions • Sometimes they do not disclose identity (anonymous)

INFLUENCER ASSIGNMENT

An influencer is someone who has built forth an audience, naturally and over time, and is viewed as an authority figure on a certain subject, area, or perspective in the online space. In addition, influencers have the presence and trust in their community to persuade audiences to take a specific action based on what they share.

These individuals bring forth unique experiences, perspectives, and brand voices to the table, which makes it difficult to categorize each influencer in a consistent way.

You are asked to create a report on the top influencers for

- Your university

- A sports or athletic team

- A local business or nonprofit

- An established brand

In your assignment, you will need to provide each of the following:

- *Overview.* Introduce your focus for this influencer report (university, sports and athletic team, etc.).

- *Current influencer marketing status.* Provide an overview of the influencer relationship status (has the client done an influencer marketing plan before? What has worked and not worked in the past?).

- *Opportunities and challenges with influencer marketing.* What are some of the challenges facing brands with influencers? What are some of the opportunities?

- *Goal and focus for influencer marketing.* Why is it important to create this partnership? How does this tie to business, communication, and marketing objectives?

- *List of recommended influencers* (use the tools in Chapter 8 of *Social Media for Strategic Communication* to identify at least five influencers based on location, industry, and interest) for your focused client. Provide a rationale for choosing these influencers based on your tool analysis. Which brands have they worked for before on campaigns? What is their area of interest? Which social media platform are they more established on?

- *Analysis of each influencer.* Analyze the influencers and determine if they are "real influencers" or "fake influencers":
  - Are they actually publishing their knowledge openly rather than just getting paid endorsements?
  - Is their network made up of fellow colleagues or other influencers that help create a mutually beneficial relationship?
  - Are they focused on their numbers rather than the connections to and health of their communities?

- ○ Do they have the experience and ability to show the evidence of their work through measureable results based on what they are preaching?

- ○ Are they creating, curating, and engaging with content related to their business, or are they promoting just themselves?

- *Analysis of the content for the influencers.* Present and analyze at least two pieces of content for each influencer (a total of six pieces of content).

- *Recommendations for engaging with the influencers.* How will you establish a relationship? What metrics will you use to determine whether or not they are successful for your client?

- *References for your citations.* Make sure to cite your references for this assignment.

9 CREATING, MANAGING, AND CURATING CONTENT

You are approached by a local business to help with its content creation strategy game. The organization is particularly looking for pieces of content that will help it (1) create more brand awareness for the local market, (2) establish new relationship opportunities with the community, (3) emphasize its brand voice online, and (4) grow its online community.

You will need to

- Analyze what type of content the business is already creating (view for the past month) on the major platforms

- Discuss what two other businesses in town are doing on social media (Are they doing well on content creation? Which channels are their strongest? What are some gaps to note for this business to take advantage of?)

- Look at what metrics can be analyzed from the content (reactions, retweets, favorites, comments, etc.) and evaluate what the business has already done and what it can improve on

- Propose certain content ideas for the business's social media channels (What three platforms would you like to use and feel is relevant for this business? Review the table as follows for sample ideas.)

- Create sample updates and mock-ups of three messages for each platform (for a total of nine messages):
  - Highlight the content that will be created.
  - Write the message and copy for the content that will be shared on the designated platform.
  - Discuss what metrics you will use to analyze whether this content was successful or not.

Platform	Platform Characteristics	Content Ideas
Facebook	• Max character limit is 63,206, but posts that have 80 characters have the most engagement (Jackson, 2017).	• Start an update with a question • End an update with a question • Create a list • Add a quote from an article, interview, feature, or event/speaker • Update with emojis • Use an image with text overlay • Attribute and tag other accounts • Provide a customized URL
Twitter	• There is a 280-character limit, but options are available to add images, videos, collages, and tag users now. • You do not always have to use all 280 characters.	• Place comments before headline • Place comments after headline • Commentary and quote of tweet • Place tweets inside the comments • Integrate multimedia • Conduct polls • Attribute with tag • Tag accounts in image or video
Instagram	• Posts have a 2,200-character limit. • Use hashtags (no more than a few) to highlight the key words and communities you want to reach.	• Tutorials • Micro-visual blogging • Giveaways and contests • Asking a question and probing for engagement • Features • Tips and tricks • Q&As • Historical features • Interviews • Updates • Behind-the-scenes • Storyboards (posts and Instagram Stories)
LinkedIn	• Posts have a 600-character max.	• Post an update • Post an update with a URL • Share a Pulse article • Post an update with an image

Resource: Jackson, D. (2017, May 22). Know your limit: The ideal length of every social media post. *Sprout Social.* Retrieved from https://sproutsocial.com/insights/social-media-character-counter/

CONTENT CREATION ASSIGNMENT: IMAGES

You are asked to create content focused on a holiday, event, or celebration for your university.

- Introduce the background of your university. How active is it on social media? Has it created content for a certain holiday or event? What content got the most engagement? Which could have been improved?

- Discuss the background of jumping on holiday trends with social media content. What are the benefits of this? What are the challenges? Outline an example of holiday content done well, and one that did not go over that well. What two takeaways from these cases are important to note for this exercise?

- Research three holidays, events, or celebrations (National Coffee Day, National Donut Day, etc.) you would like to create content for. Discuss your rationale for creating content for these holidays, events, and celebrations.

- Explain the key audiences for this content. Highlight how this content would be relevant for your university's audience. What type of content resonates with your audience members? How often will they share this?

- Highlight the tools you will use to create these pieces of content (Adobe products, Adobe Spark, Canva, etc.).

- Discuss what platforms you will use to publish this content. Also highlight the influencers and opinion leaders to whom you will reach out to get this content in their hands and on their social media feeds.

- Write the associated copy at the end of the image. Use proper formatting and copy for all relevant content.

- Discuss how you will determine whether or not this effort was successful. Report what analytics and key performance indicators (KPIs) you will use to determine if this piece of content succeeded or not.

- Provide three sample images (for a total of nine) with updates for
  - Facebook
  - Instagram
  - Twitter

SOCIAL MEDIA CONTENT MARKETING AND ANALYTICS CERTIFICATION REPORT

Students must create a current real-world digital audit report. The analytic proposal will describe the current social media tools and metrics employed, and the student team will suggest a strategy, set business-related goals for social media, and outline a detailed plan for tracking success.

For this report, students will complete several certifications and analyze their potential and application for social media strategies for personal branding and professional campaigns:

- Hubspot Inbound Marketing Certification Program

- Brandwatch for Students Program

- HubSpot Content Marketing Certification

- Hootsuite Social Ads and/or Advanced Social Media Strategy Program

- Google Analytics

- HubSpot Social Media Certification

Components of the report include each of the following:

- Overview of the program and brand overseeing the certification

- Key lessons learned from the program

- Importance of certifications for social media (emphasis on lifelong learning and engaging in the community, etc.)

- Benefits and challenges for each certification program

- Sample work

- References

VISUAL STORYBOARD ASSIGNMENT

This assignment can be tailored to any visual platform for a campaign (Snapchat, Instagram, Facebook Messenger, etc.). The purpose is to create a visual storyboard of the content you would like to create. This can be a takeover of an account, coverage of a game or event, or even strategic alignment of a story to help your personal brand.

NAME: _____

PROJECT/CAMPAIGN: _____

OBJECTIVE: _____

AUDIENCE: _____

DATE: _____

Visual:		Visual:		Visual:		Visual:	
Time:		Time:		Time:		Time:	
Audio:		Audio:		Audio:		Audio:	
Script:		Script:		Script:		Script:	
Visual:		Visual:		Visual:		Visual:	
Time:		Time:		Time:		Time:	
Audio:		Audio:		Audio:		Audio:	
Script:		Script:		Script:		Script:	

EVALUTION: _____

BEST PRACTICES: _____

LIST OF TOOLS:

- Equipment

- Content creation tools

- Measurement tools and KPIs

SOCIAL MEDIA WORKSHOP ASSIGNMENT

You are asked to create and lead a social media workshop on a specific current topic, area of specialization, or area of expertise you feel you have to offer to the class. Many social media professionals host (and charge for) workshop sessions on specific topics at local, national, and even global events.

You will only have 20 minutes to deliver the social media workshop. Essentially, you want to dedicate a minute to each slide, so you will want to include about 20 slides. These workshops must have a consistent theme and be formatted professionally.

Ideally, you want to focus on a topic that you find (1) would be beneficial for your audience, (2) showcases your interests and expertise, and (3) could be used as a sample talk for future speaking engagements.

Suggested areas to focus on for a workshop include but are not limited to the following (other proposed topics need permission from your professor):

- Facebook paid ads: How to create and analyze them

- WeChat and WhatsApp

- Trials and tribulations of live video

- Snapchat strategy

- Business networking with LinkedIn

- All about the filter: Creating visual content on Instagram

- How to create and engage in a Twitter chat

- Instagram Stories: Strategies 101

- Video creation for social media

- Influencer marketing

- Social media crisis communications

- Social media and sports/entertainment/nonprofits

FORMAT FOR WORKSHOP

- Introduction (1 slide): Title of workshop.

- Introduction of speaker (1 slide): An overview of who you are, whom you represent, and your contact information.

- Agenda (1 slide): Set the pace for your audience and outline what will be covered, which deliverables will be discussed, and time for Q&A.

- Content (10+ slides): Make sure the slides and workshop are visual and full of information. Integrate insights, research (with proper citations), best practices, case studies, and campaigns. You can even do an exercise with the members of your audience if you want to help them be part of the experience (bonus!).

- Call to action (5 slides): Leave the audience with steps to take based on the information you have provided. Make one recommendation for each slide. Integrate a visual to illustrate your point.

- Summary (1 slide): Briefly summarize what to do next.

- Resources (1 slide): Share a list of resources (articles, books, people to follow, hashtags and accounts to follow on social media, etc.) with your audience.

- Closing/Q&A (1 slide): List your contact information and open up the workshop for questions.

PROMOTION OF WORKSHOP

- Think about how to promote your workshop. Some ideas include a Snapchat Geofilter, a Twitter hashtag, promoted ads targeting audiences to come and see your workshop, and scheduling a live video on Facebook, Twitter, or Instagram.

- *You are your best spokesperson!* Make sure to share this and get engagement on your own personal social media accounts. Discuss how you will do this and how you will make sure to create buzz, excitement, and word-of-mouth communications about your workshop. Also, think about who in your group could serve as influencers to help pass along this workshop experience with their network. Reach out to your community to think about who could do this effectively.

PRESENTATION

- You will want to brand your presentation and workshop, and also make sure it is tailored to *your* voice as a social media professional. Consider looking at presentation templates (Canva, Adobe Spark, etc.) to think of ways to integrate your personal brand (create a logo, make a call-to-action statement, include a slide with contact information, etc.).

- Make sure not to have too much text on your slides. Think visual, but also provide enough information so your audience will not have to write everything down.

- Integrate multimedia and visuals into the mix. Photos and videos are visuals, but so is text. Be creative and innovative with this.

DELIVERABLES

- Resources can be delivered either as a hard copy or digitally (Google Docs, QR code, personal website, etc.).
  - Have a SlideDeck (or PowerPoint, InDesign, Keynote, etc.) presentation available for audiences to download.
  - Include one page of resources.
  - Include a one-page handout summarizing key parts (an infographic is acceptable).

CONTENT CREATION AND CURATION AUDIT EXERCISE

You are starting out in your career to create a brand for yourself and for your company. You have to create original content, but also align it with who you are and your brand voice.

Even in content creation and curation, you must be aware of the competitors and what they are doing. You are asked to create a content creation and curation audit in which you will analyze, outline, and discuss your major competitors in your content area on social media through a thorough SWOT (strengths, weaknesses, opportunities, and threats) analysis.

Content Creation Components	You	Competitor 1	Competitor 2	Competitor 3	Analysis (rank each member from 1, *strong*, to 5, *weak*, and provide a rationale)
Brand Voice	• How would you define your voice in the content you share?				
Industry/Social Media Area	• List the areas you focus on (Instagram and fashion, food, and travel, etc.)				
Content Platforms	• List the platforms you use (e.g., blogs, Twitter, and Instagram)				
Type of Content	• Videos • Blogs • Stories • Updates • Communities • Articles • What is the overall tone when creating the content? Is it tied to brand voice?				

Content Creation Components	You _____	Competitor 1 _____	Competitor 2 _____	Competitor 3 _____	Analysis (rank each member from 1, *strong*, to 5, *weak*, and provide a rationale)
Original Content	• What is your best-performing content? • What are influencer reactions? Who are the biggest advocates for content?				
Curation Content (frequency/type)	• How frequently are you posting and sharing content? Are you adding in your own comments or just sharing a link or article? Are you using a personalized URL shortener?				
Audience Reaction (feedback/ influence/ engagement)	• Are there lots of shares and feedback? Comments? Likes? • Does your content get no response or shares? • What does this mean?				
Results/ Recommendations (How will you work to address these points in your own content and curation strategy?)					

10 MEASUREMENT, EVALUATION, BUDGET, AND CALENDAR

PAID MEDIA ASSIGNMENT: FACEBOOK AND INSTAGRAM

You want to create a mock-up of a Facebook and Instagram ad to reach recruiters for your dream job after graduation. This is an opportunity for you to create paid media content to promote your brand to possible audiences you want to reach.

You will need to

- Go to www.facebook.com/ads/creativehub. This is where you will get access to the Facebook Creative Hub outlet. Sign in to your Facebook account.

- See the options to create various mock-ups. For this assignment, you will need to create *two* mockups to share via Facebook, and *two* for Instagram.

- Create mock-ups once you decide which ones to do (e.g., Instagram has several options).

- Review the resources Facebook Creative Hub provides (e.g., Get Inspired) to see what has worked in the past for brands, companies, and others. This could help you brainstorm some ideas.

ASSIGNMENT COMPONENTS

- Discuss the rise in paid media within social media. Why is this relevant for social media professionals to note? Where does paid media fall into the scope of social media strategy? Provide references and evidence (e.g., citations to research) to support your points.

- Provide an overview of Facebook and Instagram, including current statistics, characteristics, and trends on these sites related to paid media.

- Highlight which ad mock-ups you will be creating for this assignment.

- Create the mock-ups and provide a rationale for why you created them.

- Discuss the audience, target areas, and overall measurement requirements needed for these pieces of content (provide estimates for a budget).

- Outline the time and cost for each ad (a few days, a week, etc.).

MOCK-UPS TO CHOOSE FROM FOR AD ASSIGNMENT

Facebook	Instagram
• Facebook Carousel	• Instagram Stories
• Facebook Canvas	• Instagram Image
• Facebook Image	• Instagram Video
• Facebook Video	• Instagram Carousel
• Facebook 360 Video	
• Facebook Frame	

STEPS TO TAKE FOR THIS ASSIGNMENT

Step 1: Create a title for your mock-up and set up your profile name. Select the profile picture you want to use.

Step 2: Choose the ad content (image, video, etc.) and make sure to follow the ad guidelines. Add in the copy you want to have here for your piece of content.

Step 3: Create and download your ad mock-up. Make sure to test this both on your computer and on mobile.

Step 4: Outline the payment strategy you will set forth for this piece of content. Determine the paid measurements you will need to use and report to determine if this piece of content is successful.

Step 5: Discuss the ethical and legal implications and practices to be aware of when it comes to ads on each of these platforms. What steps will you take to make sure to follow these guidelines?

SOCIAL MEDIA BUDGET ASSIGNMENT

One of the hardest things to do for a social media campaign is to justify the work for a social media initiative or educational training session. Make sure you provide sound estimates, details of the materials and tools needed, and a rationale for this investment. Along with accounting for the cost of tools, time, data, measurement, and education, providing a rationale for why these are necessary is key.

You have been asked to create and justify a budget for a

- Social media campaign

- Influencer marketing campaign

- Creative execution plan for a new platform

Make sure you account for all of the associated costs for tools, time, management, and analysis of data; content creation (tools, talent, time, etc.); and necessary educational training. Justify your points for each cost associated with each section of your budget.

The following is a brief template for creating a budget. Tailor this appropriately for the overall focus of your social media plan or specific initiative.

Objective 1:					
Strategy					
	Details	**Quantity**	**Cost**	**Total Projected**	**Rationale**
Tactic 1					
Tactic 2					
Measurement					
Content Creation					
Education and Training					
Objective 1 Cost					
Objective 2:					
Strategy					
	Details	**Quantity**	**Cost**	**Total Projected**	**Rationale**
Tactic 1					
Tactic 2					
Measurement					

(Continued)

(Continued)

Objective 2:					
Strategy					
	Details	Quantity	Cost	Total Projected	Rationale
Content Creation					
Education and Training					
Objective 2 Total					
Objective 3:					
Strategy					
	Details	Quantity	Cost	Total Projected	Rationale
Tactic 1					
Tactic 2					
Measurement					
Content Creation					
Education and Training					
Objective 3 Cost					
Total Cost					

CONTENT CREATION ASSIGNMENT: EVALUATION

You are asked to evaluate a set of tools and applications for your internship, and present your findings to your internship coordinator and his or her supervisor.

Your task is to work as a group to analyze and evaluate these tools. Once you have completed your evaluation, note which tools you'd recommend investing in or using.

Your presentation should be no more than 10 minutes long. Present a one-sheet outline and/or infographic for your presentation with the highlights.

In your presentation to the class, prepare

- A slide deck (PowerPoint, Keynote, Adobe Illustrator, Adobe Spark Page, Prezi, etc.) to showcase your findings

- A set of tools to focus on from the following content creation categories:
  - Photo/image
  - Video
  - Written
  - Audio

- An outline of the presentation
  - Overview of the content creation category you have decided to focus on
  - Overview of the tools that will be discussed in this presentation (highlight three in the category you choose from)
  - Features and unique characteristics of the tool
  - The brand that made the tool.
  - Price point differences (free, paid, premium, etc.)
  - Evaluation of each tool and its benefits and challenges
  - A summary with your recommendations and choice

11 HOW SOCIAL MEDIA IS APPLIED: EXPLORING DIFFERENT SPECIALIZATIONS, PART I

SOCIAL MEDIA AND SPORTS ASSIGNMENT

You are asked to create a game plan for social media activities for a local sports team. Your job is to research this team's current use of social media content, brand voice, and engagement across its social media platforms.

Make sure to include the following in your analysis:

- *Overview of the sports team.* What is the team's background, history, and connection to the community?

- *Current state of the team's social media presence.* How engaged is the team online? Does it have a designated handle that is consistent across all channels? Which channel is most engaged with the community? Which channel needs improvement?
  - *Highlight recent cases of teams who have benefited from social media* (Loyola-Chicago for the 2018 NCAA Basketball Tournament, the Houston Astros for the 2017 World Series, Chloe Kim from the 2018 Winter Olympics, etc.).

- *Brand voice on social media.* What is the overall tone for the team's social media accounts? What has it done previously?

- *Previous social media coverage of games, players, and staff.* What has the team done before? What worked or did not work? What are some opportunities and new tools to test out?
  - *Analyze the team's social media presence.* What is its brand voice? How engaged is the team with fans?
  - *Analyze the players' social media platforms* (top players). Which platform do they use? What content do they share? How would you define their brand voice?
    - Identify one team and one player for each platform (Facebook, Twitter, Instagram, YouTube, etc.) that do a good job with their brand voice and personal brand, and discuss how the team and player have benefited from social media. What lessons can we learn from them?

- *Proposed game plan.* Pick a game that is happening and outline a game plan for what content should be sent out and at what time. Propose a mixture of different updates from video, images, and text. Be creative but strategic in understanding the team's overall tone of voice on social media. Create your proposed game plan for the event. Highlight the platforms that will be used (based on your analysis of the team's previous social media platform use) and pieces of content you want to share out at certain times.

- *Measurement and evaluation.* Discuss what metrics you will use to determine whether or not this is effective for the event on social media.

- *Highlight best practices and future steps to take on social media.* What are some recommendations you have for the team in the future? What are some tools or platforms the team needs to be aware of?

- *Bonus.* Share your proposal with the team you have chosen for additional feedback.

SOCIAL MEDIA AND CRISIS COMMUNICATION MESSAGE MAPPING ASSIGNMENT

You are asked to create a message map for your client as part of its social media crisis communication plan. Make sure to outline which potential crises your client could experience (brand, nonprofit, university, client for class, etc.), and outline the key audience(s) that are relevant to target for this particular situation. Discuss which social media channels you will use, the main key points you want to communicate with the client, and what types of content you want to create to be part of the key messages. Last, discuss how you will evaluate the effectiveness of these messages on social media and your recommendations for the future.

For a sample message plan, check out the Centers for Disease Control and Prevention's Crisis & Emergency Risk Communication message mapping template.

Situation	Audiences	Channel(s)	Key Messages (Primary and Secondary)	Pieces of Content (Multimedia, Images, Links, etc.)	Evaluation	Recommendations
Crisis 1					• Listening metrics, monitoring, etc.	
Crisis 2						
Crisis 3						
Crisis 4						
Crisis 5						

SOCIAL MEDIA AND JOURNALISM ASSIGNMENTS AND EXERCISES

Social media and journalism have become integrated, and you will want to propose and showcase the power of social media within this specialized industry for this assignment.

- *Class newsroom.* The class is designated as a newsroom, where specific pieces of content need to be shared, created, and distributed at certain times. Students will need to pitch the professor with story ideas on what they would like to create for the class newsroom, and then be responsible for creating the content. Students will be responsible for

  - Writing content to be shared on social media (e.g., a video or written story posted online)

  - Proposing updates about the content to gain traction

  - Evaluating and measuring the analytics for the content of the stories, and reporting these to the professor

- *Analysis of news outlet.* You are tasked to analyze three different media outlets to determine their overall social media coverage and strategy. These can be global, national, or local media outlets.

  - Mainstream (ABC, CBS, NBC, etc.)

  - Industry specific (TechCrunch, Mashable, The Next Web, Cheddar, etc.)

  - Individual based (reporter, anchor, YouTuber, etc.)

Make sure to analyze what the news outlet is doing as far as platform use, shared content, and pros and cons of its activity on the platforms. At the end, provide your analysis of the news outlet's current standing, and what areas it needs to improve on. Provide screenshots of each host company's social media accounts.

Type of News	Host Company	Types of Platforms Used	Shared Content	Pros	Cons	Current Status (from 1, *needs improvement*, to 5, *expert*)
Mainstream						
Industry Specific						
Individual						
ANALYSIS						

12 HOW SOCIAL MEDIA IS APPLIED: EXPLORING DIFFERENT SPECIALIZATIONS, PART II

SOCIAL MEDIA AND NONPROFIT ASSIGNMENTS AND EXERCISES

A lot of opportunities are available for nonprofits to utilize social media. The following exercises can be utilized and focused on nonprofit work with social media:

- *Create a micro-campaign focused on supporting a nonprofit's cause.* Research a local nonprofit and provide suggestions on how it can provide more engagement on its social media channels.

- *Propose an interactive and/or live video to share online.* The media in question will be video, but you have to (1) choose a cause or nonprofit to support, (2) create a video that allows people to create their own experience, and (3) once someone creates a video, determine what will motivate him or her to donate.

- *Analyze crowdfunding sites and propose a recommendation for a campaign.* Analyze features of Facebook, GoFundMe, and other platforms and see which ones are the best for crowdfunding donations and supporting causes. Provide your recommendation and rationale.

- *Propose a new initiative a nonprofit could utilize to accomplish its set objectives.* Review what strategies and campaigns the organization has implemented in the past, and consider providing some ideas on what it could do to create more buzz for its work, generate excitement and support, and create more awareness of its efforts in the community. Some ideas include

  - Organizing and conducting an influencer event campaign to generate buzz

  - Establishing a networking event for students, professionals, and others to meet local nonprofits

  - Creating a hackathon session to brainstorm ideas for a nonprofit during a 24-hour period

- *Propose a one-day social media fund-raising event.* Choose three local nonprofits, and reach out to them about a possible fund-raising initiative via social media. Establish protocols and call-to-action steps for how to donate to the cause. Create three separate messages to promote the cause:

- A video on the fund-raising initiative
- An email and letter campaign
- Visual branded content

SOCIAL CARE ASSIGNMENT

Customer service is one of the most important elements of being on the front lines for social media professionals. How you engage and interact with audience members on social media can be the difference between establishing proactive relationships and damaging audiences to the point of outrage.

OVERVIEW OF THE ASSIGNMENT

- *Define social care.* What are the benefits of having a strong social care program? What are the current practices, views, and applications of social care? Why is it important?

- *Lead by example.* Identify two brands and accounts that are proactive in social care. What are they doing well?

- *Learn from mistakes.* Identify two brands and accounts that show the consequences of not having a sound social care plan. Describe three takeaways from these case studies.

- *Identify the current customer service management tools.* Which ones are the most appropriate to use for social care? Outline three management tools and their benefits, challenges, and features.

- *Consider this current scenario.* You are the social media care professional for American Airlines, and you found out your flights from Dallas to Los Angeles have been delayed due to a service pig getting out on the plane. Many passengers, including two Instagram influencers, have started sharing updates and videos, and the story has been picked up by the news.

- *Determine the action steps.* What actions will you take to handle this situation? Outline the steps needed to address the situation.
  - *Create a social care policy* for your team members.
  - *Create three responses* for each social media platform in regard to this situation.

- *Provide references* in APA (American Psychological Association) style.

SOCIAL MEDIA AROUND THE WORLD ASSIGNMENT

It is important to understand different platforms around the world. This assignment focuses on identifying a social media platform that is prominent in another country. Research and identify a region that has used a social media platform other than the main ones (e.g., Facebook, Twitter, Instagram, Snapchat, LinkedIn, and YouTube).

You are asked to create a report and workshop presentation for the class about this platform.

ASSIGNMENT GUIDELINES

- *Overview of the country.* Identify key characteristics, historical events, current media, and the digital/social media landscape. What are some previous campaigns and social media initiatives that have been implemented in this country?

- *Overview of the platform.* What are the key characteristics of this platform? What type of platform is it, and what is the current user base? Describe the use, behaviors, and pieces of content being created and initiated on the platform. How would you describe the platform's audience?

- *Characteristics of the platform.* How is the platform used? What have been the significant updates and uses? Which brands, campaigns, and individuals have used this platform positively? What have been some of the challenges? What have been some of the successes? Highlight two cases that can serve as examples.

- *Application of the platform.* Discuss how the platform in this country is used, and how it might be used in your country. Discuss the challenges, opportunities, and best practices needed to use this platform.

- *Creative execution of the platform.* Provide three possible ways to use this platform in your country. Identify how you would educate and train users and implement the use of this platform.

- *References.* Make sure to provide your citations in APA style.

13

WHAT DOES THE SOCIAL MEDIA WORLD HAVE THAT IS NEW?

FUTURE TRENDS PITCH ASSIGNMENT

You are tasked with educating, informing, and reporting to your team about the latest new trend hitting the industry in social media and emerging media. You have 10–12 minutes to present an overview in a SlideDeck presentation to the class.

Along with the SlideDeck, create a one-sheet handout to share with your classmates (hard copy and digital).

Make sure to provide the following information for your team:

- *Overview.* What future trend are you discussing, and what key definitions does your team need to know? When did the buzz about this trend first start? Who (influencer, media outlet, brand, etc.) got everyone's attention about this new trend?

  - *Bonus.* Conduct a monitoring and listening trend analysis to show data and evidence on how people are talking about this trend. Show the data in your handout and presentation.

- *Core characteristics.* Why are people paying attention to this trend? How is this different than others in the industry? Compare this trend with two others happening right now.

- *Pros and cons.* What are the pros and cons for this trend? Outline three pros and three cons for this trend.

- *Case studies.* Outline two or three examples of this trend being used or implemented in a campaign. What were the results? What are some lessons to take away from this?

- *Recommendation.* What do you recommend for this trend? Should your team invest in it or not? What action steps should the team take?

- *References.* Cite your sources in APA (American Psychological Association) style.

SOCIAL MEDIA CHECKLIST FOR CONTINUED EDUCATION

You have finished the social media book and class (congrats!). However, learning does not end in the classroom. In this industry, you have to continue to be on top of things and learn new tools, techniques, areas, and even platforms. This assignment will give you a chance to outline what areas you would like to work in after completing your social media class, training, and program.

Goal: _____

Deadline for accomplishment: _____

Benefits of continued education: _____

Evaluation of continued education program: _____

Professional Based	Continued Education	Networking	Personal Brand

☐ **Workshops**
☐ **Webinars**
☐ **Social media training**
  • **Certifications**
    ○ **Free**
    ○ **Paid**
☐ **Platform-based training**
☐ **Client work**
  • **Internships**
  • **Freelance**
  • **Influencer based**
  • **Collaborations**
  • **Partnerships**
☐ **Conferences (local, national, international)**
☐ **Other:** _____
	☐ Graduate school
	☐ Certifications
	☐ Workshops
	☐ Communities
	☐ Other: _____
		☐ Local events
		☐ Conferences
		☐ Groups
		☐ Chats
		☐ Find a mentor
		☐ Reach out to members in the community, industry, etc.
		☐ Professional etiquette
		☐ Join communities
		  • Platform
		  • Media
		  • Professional
		  • Influencer and advocate based
			☐ Social media audit
			  • Monthly/quarterly/year
			  • Benchmark metrics
			  • Evaluate content
			  • Identify key advocates in community
			☐ Create content
			  • Branded content
			  • Relevant personal brand topic tree items
			  • Schedule for content creation
			☐ Curate content
			  • Set up schedule for reading, evaluating, and sharing content
			  • Set up sharing schedule
			  • Use a mixture of share, share and engage, and share and ask a question to the community

Professional Based	Continued Education	Networking	Personal Brand
			☐ Partnerships • Research potential partnerships • Identify brands or causes that would be good to partner with • Identify key benefits and challenges • Reach out to organizations (set a number) • Provide a win-win scenario • Identify key impact factors and deliverables • Reflect, evaluate, and create best practices Collaborations ☐ Fellow professionals ☐ Brands ☐ Causes ☐ Interest ☐ Organizations (local, national, and international) ☐ Influencers/ community advocates ☐ Other: _____
Deadline: _____	Deadline: _____	Deadline: _____	Deadline: _____
Action Plan			

CREATIVE INNOVATION OF SOCIAL MEDIA EDUCATION: HOW TO CONTINUE BEING A LIFELONG LEARNER

Social media is all about being a lifelong learner, but it is about becoming a resource as well. Educating others and establishing your perspective in the field can open opportunities and experiences for you as a social media professional.

Ask yourself the following questions to see how you approach social media, and how creative innovation is necessary in social media education beyond the classroom.

Think about these questions, and be prepared to share your answers with the class. Provide at least three references and citations for your answers.

- Is social media a process, a skill, or both? Why or why not?

- What are your thoughts about the role you will take after this class and graduation to continue your social media education?
  - How will you continue to collaborate with and learn from others?
  - How will you continue to establish yourself in the field as a resource?
  - What steps will you take to mentor and coach others in social media? How will you approach your feedback?

- How should social media be approached?

- How can we be lifelong learners in social media?

- What should be integrated into a lifelong learning program for social media?

- What exercises will you incorporate to become a lifelong learner? Discuss the benefits and challenges of
  - Workshops
  - Role-plays
  - Hosting educational training sessions
  - Peer learning and personal learning networks
  - Simulations of social media campaigns

- What are some of your future goals in the field?

SELF-REFLECTION AND ACTUALIZATION EXERCISE

It is important to not only debrief after a lesson, assignment, or project, but also take the time to reflect on and analyze your overall performance on a project or even in a class. Answer these questions and see what steps to take in the future to continue your education in social media. This is more of a reflective exercise, but an important one to determine the next steps you will take in your social media career and education.

- How confident were you in the content from this class? What was your favorite subject?

- During this class, how well do you feel you mastered each of the following?
  - The content for the class
  - Assignments (Which assignments and exercises did you like? Which ones were challenging?)
  - Exercises on- and offline
  - Presentations (class clients, group presentations, individual presentations, client presentations, etc.)

- What were some of the biggest wins for you in the class? What did you learn or do that made you proud to achieve this?

- At the beginning of the semester, you listed some areas you were most concerned about. What was the result of the actions you decided to take during the semester to overcome these challenges?

- What was the biggest surprise for you in this class? Explain and highlight what made this your light bulb moment.

- What three things will you do to improve on the aspects of this class that were challenging for the future?

- What are three takeaways from your learning experience in this class? List three action steps you will take to continue your social media education and be self-aware of your professional activities in the industry.